MW00508770

PHARMACOLOGY AND DRUG ADDICTION

*How to Overcome Alcohol Abuse, Drug Use, and
Narcotic Substances.
Diagnosis & Treatment*

Livio Leone

© Copyright 2021 by Livio Leone - All rights reserved.

The following Book is reproduced below with the goal of providing information that is as accurate and reliable as possible. Regardless, purchasing this Book can be seen as consent to the fact that both the publisher and the author of this book are in no way experts on the topics discussed within and that any recommendations or suggestions that are made herein are for entertainment purposes only. Professionals should be consulted as needed prior to undertaking any of the action endorsed herein.

This declaration is deemed fair and valid by both the American Bar Association and the Committee of Publishers Association and is legally binding throughout the United States.

Furthermore, the transmission, duplication, or reproduction of any of the following work including specific information will be considered an illegal act irrespective of if it is done electronically or in print. This extends to creating a secondary or tertiary copy of the work or a recorded copy and is only allowed with the express written consent from the Publisher. All additional right reserved.

The information in the following pages is broadly considered a truthful and accurate account of facts and as such, any inattention, use, or misuse of the information in question by the reader will render any resulting actions solely under their purview. There are no scenarios in which the publisher or the original author of this work can be in any fashion deemed liable for any hardship or damages that may befall them after undertaking information described herein.

Additionally, the information in the following pages is intended only for informational purposes and should thus be thought of as universal. As befitting its nature, it is presented without assurance regarding its prolonged validity or interim quality. Trademarks that are mentioned are done without written consent and can in no way be considered an endorsement from the trademark holder.

TABLE OF CONTENTS

Introduction

Clinical pharmacology can be defined both as a science and as a medical specialty. As a science, it studies drugs' action on the human organism and the human organism's action on drugs, both in healthy and sick people.

As a medical specialty, clinical pharmacology is concerned, together with other medical specialties and other health professions, with achieving optimal use of drugs by increasing their efficacy and reducing their risk, i.e., rationalizing the use of drugs by choosing the most appropriate drug and administration schedule for each patient.

Diagnostic agents are considered to be those drugs that are used for the clinical diagnosis of diseases. Although they do not have a therapeutic effect on the patient's pathology, since they are not administered on a regular and scheduled basis, they are not exempt from presenting undesirable effects.

Due to their lack of therapeutic action, there has not been the awareness to consider many of them as medicines until enacting the law.

The diagnostic agent's efficacy lies in its clinical specificity and the method's sensitivity in its detection. Although they generally have a wide margin of safety, they are not exempt from presenting undesirable effects like any other drug. Finally, the drug's quality guarantees its biological behavior in the patient and the reliability of the results in establishing the clinical diagnosis.

The desire to establish a clinical diagnosis that is increasingly more objective, faster, and more bloodless for the patient has led to spectacular technological progress thanks to new detection systems and diagnostic strategies.

In some cases, this dynamic has led to incorporating existing drugs in other clinical applications, requiring their new indication to be channeled through compassionate use or clinical trials until their definitive registration. The mere fact of establishing false positive or negative diagnoses with drugs not authorized for this purpose highlights the responsibility of arguing for their correct application.

What are the pharmacological treatments?

The development of new drugs has succeeded in modifying the course of the disease:

- Modifying treatment has a preventive character. It reduces the frequency and severity of outbreaks and reduces the formation of new lesions in the brain and spinal cord. It has side effects, and the reaction to the treatment depends on each case.

- Treatment of the outbreak accelerates the recovery of symptoms after a relapse but does not modify the disease's evolution. Corticosteroids are used in these acute cases.

- Symptomatic treatment aims to treat the symptoms associated with the disease and improve quality of life.

Because of their current relevance as diagnostic agents, the drugs used are described:

- In functional tests.

- As dyes.

- As contrasts in imaging techniques.

- As radiopharmaceuticals.

Functional tests

The substances used for functional tests are agents that present diverse physio-pharmacological activities; thus, we find: Sugars such as glucose and xylose in the diagnosis of diabetes

of diabetes and permeability of the gastrointestinal tract; amino acids such as arginine, a potent stimulant of growth hormone in the pituitary gland, and the release of insulin used in the insulin release used in the diagnosis of growth hormone

of growth hormone deficiency; enzyme substrates such as fluorescein/fluorescein dilaurate used in diagnosing exocrine pancreatic insufficiency or bentiromide used in the indirect measurement of exocrine pancreatic function by assessing para-aminobenzoic acid metabolites in plasma.

Hormones and analogs such as gonadorelin for the treatment and diagnosis of hypothalamic function.

Desmopressin in the renal concentrating ability test (diabetes insipidus). Metyrapone in the test for the assessment of hypothalamic-pituitary function (Cushing's syndrome). Protirelin in hypothyroidism of central or peripheral origin, hyperthyroidism: Basedow's disease, toxic adenoma, and abnormalities in prolactin secretion. Secretin for the identification of gastrinoma and diagnosis of pancreatic function. Tetracosactide, ACTH analog, is indicated in the diagnosis of adrenal function.

Among the drugs: edrophonium for myasthenia gravis, methacholine for differential diagnosis of asthma.

Omeprazole in screening for gastroesophageal reflux. furosemide and captopril in renography. In ophthalmology, mydriatics, and cycloplegics.

Antibiotics and other drugs in hypersensitivity tests. Dipyridamole in cardiac studies. Acetazolamide in mammographic studies of the brain.

Antigens, tuberculin in the screening and diagnosis of tuberculosis, cocciodioidin in the differential diagnosis of coccidioidomycosis among other bacterial and fungal infections. Histoplasmin in histoplasmosis. Candidin in candidiasis. Other allergens used in allergic tests, such as grasses, metals, etc., have not been forgotten.

The wide range of agents used in functional tests can be verified. We have only collected, as an example, some of those that may be required from hospital pharmacy services.

1.2. Dyes

In the diagnostic and therapeutic field, various dyes have been used as markers to identify vascular spaces and physiological conduits or determine fluid flow and integrity of vessels or conduits (fistulas).

We find indocyanine green used to establish cardiac output, liver function, and examination of the choroidal vasculature in ophthalmic angiography within this group.

Indigo Carmine is used as a marker in the localization of urethral orifices during cystoscopy, urethral catheterization, and identification of ureters and fistulous communications. It is also used in amniocentesis of twins to ensure that both amniotic sacs are sampled. Methylene blue, which in addition to the treatment of methemoglobinemia, is used to detect fistulas and diagnosis of ruptured amniotic membranes.

However, its use during pregnancy is not advisable since hemolytic anemia and hyperbilirubinemia have been described in neonates exposed to methylene blue.

Toluidine blue metachromatic dye used in 1-2% solution as a rinse or for direct staining of suspicious lesions in detecting oral and pharyngeal dysplasia or carcinoma.

Eye drops or staining solutions are a handy tool in ophthalmologic diagnosis: pink Bengal and fluorescein are used in ophthalmology to identify foreign bodies and corneal integrity.

Fluorescein is also used in other examinations such as tonometry, gonioscopy, and electromyography. It is administered intravenously to evaluate iris vascularity, observation of aqueous flow, differential diagnosis of malignant, non-malignant tumors, and the determination of the time and adequacy of circulation.

Recently in cataract surgery, triptan blue has been incorporated to make the anterior lens capsule visible, reducing the risk of tears and capsulorhexis.

These and other dyes, some of them also used as food additives or antiseptics, can mark organs or areas in specific diagnostic processes or therapeutic interventions.

1.3. Diagnostic Contrasts

Diagnostic imaging is one of the most widely used methods for determining a disease's origin, condition, and evolution. The agents are used to aid in these diagnostic techniques by facilitating images obtained thanks to devices of varying complexity.

Among the agents for diagnostic imaging are contrasts for radiography, computed tomography, magnetic resonance imaging, ultrasound, and radiopharmaceuticals in Nuclear Medicine, used to visualize the body's various organs and cavities.

1.3.1. Radiology

X-rays are a highly energetic, ionizing radiation used in medicine to obtain internal organs and blood vessels' images. Tissues allow the passage of radiation depending on their density; the lower the density, the more significant the radiation that passes through them. When the body is subjected to the X-ray source, the unabsorbed radiation passes through the body and is detected by photographic film: radiography, unique screen: fluoroscopy, or through a computer: computed tomography (CT).

Computed tomography increases the diagnostic possibilities of X-rays as it allows a higher resolution. It consists of circular irradiation around the body, after which the non-absorbed radiation is collected in multiple detectors, which, transmitted to a computer, constructs a virtual digital image representing a plane or "slice.

" The integration of the various planes makes it possible to obtain a multidimensional image of the organ or tissue under study.

X-ray contrasts are characterized by containing in their structure one or more atoms of high atomic number and high density, capable of absorbing X-radiation. This type of substance makes it possible to identify structures with similar densities that could not be observed in their absence by applying them to various cavities.

Currently, the most commonly used radiopaque agents are barium contrasts and iodinated liposoluble and hydrosoluble ones.

1.3.1.1. Barium contrasts

Barium sulfate is the most widely used contrast agent in the study of digestive tract alterations. It presents high density for X-rays with minimal absorption and low cost. It is used by all (40-450 g) and rectal (150-750 g) routes and allows observing possible narrowing, ulcers, and alterations of the digestive mucosa. The use of double-contrast by administration of barium sulfate and air or carbon dioxide (bicarbonate) improves the sensitivity for examining the stomach or colon. The use of micronized barium sulfate improves the capacity to detect ulcers compared to conventional barium sulfate.

Its most relevant adverse effects are gastrointestinal alterations and anaphylaxis in sensitive patients. It cannot be administered in case of suspected intestinal obstruction and perforation.

Its administration by aspiration into the bronchial system may cause dyspnea and pneumonitis. Intravenous administration causes arrhythmias of varying degrees from ventricular fibrillation to asystole and death by cardiac arrest.

Due to the low sensitivity of barium sulfate and radiography (66%), its indications are limited, and other diagnostic procedures are used.

Other diagnostic procedures such as endoscopy or nuclear medicine are used. However, it is being used successfully in gastrointestinal MRI and CT.

1.3.1.2. Iodinated Contrasts

Iodinated contrasts base their activity on the content of iodine atoms. They are organic salts of triiodinated benzoic acid derivatives, which gives them minimal reactivity and the possibility of modulating their water solubility-lipophilicity and consequently their pharmacokinetics. Their minimal reactivity allows them to be administered intravenously and in various cavities such as the genitourinary system, and some of them can even be used in myelography.

The most relevant aspects related to iodinated contrasts are:

- Radiodensity, which depends on the relative amount of iodine per molecule, determines their efficacy.

Viscosity is another determinant of efficacy since it affects the time during which an organ or vessel will be exposed to the iodinated radiopaque agent's effects. It will also affect the speed of administration, especially when small caliber catheters are used.

- Osmolarity, which depends on the number of particles present in a given volume.

This has been related to the incidence of adverse effects. Ionic derivatives upon dissociation (producing twice as many particles in the same volume) will present a higher osmolarity for the same iodine content, presenting more significant toxicity. Some contrast agents can form molecular aggregates reducing the number of particles present in solution and consequently a lower osmolarity.

- Iodinated contrast agents are traditionally classified into high osmolarity ionic, low osmolarity ionic, and nonionic. This grouping includes agents with similar toxicity profiles and areas of application.

- High osmolarity ionic contrast agents are the sodium and meglumine salts of triiodinated benzoic acid at concentrations ranging from 40-70%.

These include sodium amidotrizoate, sodium and meglumine amidotrizoate, and sodium and meglumine iothalamate.

They are indicated in urography and angiography by conventional radiography or computed tomography in persons with low risk of suffering anaphylactic reactions, and hemodynamically stable since their high osmolarity (600-1000 mOsm/l) will condition a vasovagal response that can produce hypotension due to vasodilatation.

- Low osmolarity ionic contrasts have only one representative, a compound of the sodium and meglumine salts of ioxaglic acid.

It is a dimeric compound of triiodobenzoic acid, has six atoms of iodine per molecule, is used at concentrations of 20-40%, and has an osmolarity of 600 mOsm/kg, which confers a lower risk of vasovagal response.

It can be administered by intravenous, urinary, joint, and uterine routes and can be considered the agent of choice in urography and angiography in patients at high risk of adverse reactions (history of asthma, allergy to iodinated contrasts, hemodynamically unstable or treated with beta-blockers or interleukin).

- Low osmolarity nonionic contrasts are triiodobenzoic acid amides and therefore do not dissociate in solution.

They are used at concentrations of 30-40% and have an osmolarity of 600 mOsm/kg.

Because of their low neurotoxicity, some of them, e.g., iohexol, can be administered subarachnoid and used in myelography.

Otherwise, they can be used in all indications in which the contrasts of the previous groups could be used, but their higher cost means that they are reserved for higher-risk patients to obtain a cost-effective use.

In this group, we find iohexol, iopamidol, iopentol, iopromide, ioversol. The latter is a dimeric compound with a lower osmolarity than the previous ones for iodine concentration.

The adverse effects of iodinated contrasts are traditionally grouped as follows:

- Mild: mild nausea and vomiting, urticaria, the sensation of heat, flushing, injection site pain, and isolated premature ventricular contractions.

- Moderate: severe vomiting, edema of the face or pharynx, bronchospasm, dyspnea, chills, chest and abdominal pain, and headache.

- Severe: syncope, convulsions, pulmonary edema, shock, severe cardiac arrhythmias, and cardiorespiratory arrest.

It has been shown that high osmolarity iodinated contrast agents have a higher incidence of mild or moderate adverse effects than low osmolarity ones, but no significant differences could be established when considering severe adverse effects.

All these agents' efficacy depends on the amount of iodine, which will be similar in all of them since they can be used at different concentrations; therefore, the determining factors for using one or the other will be their toxicity profile and cost.

1.3.2. Nuclear Magnetic Resonance Imaging

Nuclear magnetic resonance (NMR) bases the creation of the image on the emission of a signal by the nuclei of the hydrogen atoms of the organism, when they return to their original alignment when, after having been subjected to a magnetic field and a low-frequency emission, they have been vibrating in a position different from the original one. The emission of the signal detected and interpreted by a computer constructs a virtual image based on the concentration and distribution of hydrogen atoms in the tissue or organ being analyzed.

As bone tissue has a low proportion of hydrogen compared to other organism tissues, it will not interfere with the soft tissues' image. The result is the production of high-resolution anatomical images used especially for neurological, muscular, or joint examinations, although the range of indications increases daily as the cost of the necessary equipment decreases.

To improve the quality of the images obtained, substances containing paramagnetic atoms can be used. These, when subjected to magnetic fields, reach high magnetic moments that will affect the response of the hydrogen nuclei of the water atoms close to the agent, increasing the signal when they return to the original alignment. This provides better quality images.

The preparation of various derivatives makes it possible to have specific agents for specific organs or tissues.

Depending on the paramagnetic atom, we find gadolinium derivatives: gadopentetic acid, gadodiamide, gadoteric acid, and gadoteridol; iron derivatives: iron III ammonium citrate, ferumoxide, and iron III oxide; and magnesium derivatives: mangafodipyr, gadodipyr, and gadoteridol.

Gadolinium derivatives can be used to diagnose brain, spinal cord, and whole-body pathologies, including craniofacial, cervical, thoracic, abdominal, breast, pelvis, locomotor system, and evaluation of renal function. Intravenous gadopentetic acid has been the reference agent in MRI, but it has a high osmolarity and is less well tolerated than the new derivatives. Orally, it is used in the diagnosis of digestive tract pathologies.

Iron derivatives are used for different indications depending on the compound: iron III ammonium citrate, used orally, allows visualization of the upper abdomen.

Ferumoxide also administered orally, is used to frame the entire abdominal digestive tract and make it possible to identify pancreatic disease, lymph nodes, and tumors. Iron II oxide, which can be administered intravenously, is used in the detection of liver tumors.

Magnafodipir is used in the diagnosis of metastatic liver disease or hepatocellular carcinoma.

The most severe adverse effects of the contrasts used in MRI, although infrequent, are anaphylactic reactions. Other adverse effects to paramagnetic agents

include flushing, heat at the injection site, dizziness, headache, nausea and vomiting, and very rarely convulsions.

Gadolinium salts administered intravenously are contraindicated in patients with pacemakers, vascular valves (contraindication for MRI), and hemolytic anemia.

Those administered orally are contraindicated in acute inflammatory bowel disease, intestinal perforation, and acute abdominal surgery.

Orally administered iron and manganese derivatives are contraindicated in case of perforation or obstruction of the gastrointestinal tract.

1.3.3. Ultrasound

Ultrasound imaging is based on the reflection produced by organs and tissues of ultrasound waves. A transducer emits the waves on the organ or tissue under examination. Its reflection, recovered by the same transducer, emits impulses to a computer that will construct an image that can be reproduced through a program on paper or a television monitor.

In general, the images produced by ultrasound are of lower quality than those produced by CT or MRI.

However, ultrasound has the advantages of being a harmless technique to the patient and can be used in obstetrics and critically ill patients, and the necessary equipment is substantially cheaper than the other techniques.

There is a modality, Doppler ultrasound, which allows the study of vascular integrity and functionalism. This technique is based on the change in sound frequency when reflected by a moving body. In this technique, the ultrasonic light beam (of known initial frequency) is reflected by a moving element, such as blood within the heart and vessels.

In ultrasound, agents can also increase the usefulness of ultrasound images and perform selective scans of specific organs and tissues.

These agents act by increasing the echo emitted by the organs or tissues they have been introduced and have allowed the development of echocardiography, abdominal ultrasound, and small superficial organs such as the thyroid, testicles, and parotids.

The most commonly used substance in ultrasound has been the association of palmitic acid and galactose, mainly used in echocardiography. More recently, human albumin microspheres in which octal fluor propane has been introduced have been introduced. These generate mighty echoes and are used primarily in opacification and blood flow determination in cardiac chambers and visualization of heart wall motion.

Galactose is contraindicated in patients with galactosemia and should be used with caution, taking into account the osmotic load in patients with functional grade IV heart failure. Adverse effects include the sensation of pain or heat at the injection site due to the vascular endothelium's irritation. Other effects include taste alterations, dyspnea, blood pressure alterations, headaches, and hypersensitivity reactions.

Albumin microspheres with octa-fluoro propane are contraindicated in patients with hypersensitivity to albumin and patients with pulmonary hypertension. Particular caution should be exercised in patients with severe cardiac, pulmonary, renal, and hepatic disease.

In summary, the use of one technique or another in diagnostic imaging depends, on the one hand, on its safety and diagnostic capacity and, on the other, on its cost-benefit ratio.

The less specific techniques are generally used more economically in screening processes and the more specific ones in more conclusive phases of the diseases' definitive diagnosis.

Chapter 1
Early Signs of Drug Addiction

Signs that somebody is mishandling drugs incorporate conduct changes like loss of enthusiasm for exercises, withdrawal from family, state of mind swings, and diminished execution busy working or school. Different signs are physical, for example, changes in dozing and dietary patterns, poor cleanliness, shaking, slurred discourse, or poor coordination. Ordinarily mishandled drugs additionally cause increasingly explicit indications. Perceiving drug misuse indications is significant for finding support and keeping away from addiction and other negative results.

Drug misuse is an intense issue with extensive results. Maltreatment of a drug is any abuse, including utilizing a drug to adapt to negative feelings or self-sedate for psychological maladjustment, utilizing an illegal or professionally prescribed drug to get high, or utilizing a physician recommended drug in a manner other than how it was proposed. There are some trademark social and physical indications of drug maltreatment just as unmistakable signs to maltreatment of various drug classes.

Manhandling drugs can prompt addiction, which is hard to treat. It is essential to perceive indications of misuse so the individual manhandling drugs can get help sooner. Proficient treatment isn't only for addiction. Anybody manhandling drugs can profit by devoted treatment to change practices and to abstain from getting dependent and the entirety of the repercussions that accompany addiction.

How to tell on the off chance that somebody is Utilizing Drugs?

Social Indications of Drug Misuse

If somebody is manhandling drugs, hope to see social changes. Despite the kind of drug, substance misuse, as a rule, makes huge adjustments to how somebody typically carries on. A large number of these are regular practices that a great many people manhandling substances display. However, everybody is extraordinary, and any new, uncommon conduct or that can't be clarified by something different, similar to a disease or an awful encounter, ought to be cause for concern. These are a portion of the more typical signs that somebody is mishandling drugs:

Issues are seeing someone. Drug misuse can cause a ton of contention in families and couples, prompting battles and separations. Connections grinding away and with companions may likewise endure.

Legitimate and money related issues. A drug propensity can be costly, and it is likewise unlawful. Mishandling drugs can prompt overspending, venturing into the red, maximizing Visas, obtaining excessively, and issuing the law.

They are lessening in execution. The modified expression that drugs make can prompt a drop in execution grinding away or at school, even in somebody who ordinarily exceeds expectations.

Disregard of obligations. Somebody who is manhandling drugs is frequently more centered on the drugs than on different obligations to family and at home.

Social withdrawal. Drug misuse frequently drives individuals to conceal their exercises from loved ones, which can eventually prompt withdrawal and minimal social contact.

Absence of inspiration and changes in the deduction. While manhandling drugs, an individual may get indifferent and uninterested in achieving a lot of anything. They may likewise battle to recall things, decide, or think regularly.

Dangerous practices. Drug misuse can lead an individual to do things the person typically wouldn't—hazardous or dangerous, such as taking, driving impaired, or having unprotected sex.

Irregular state of mind changes. A drug can affect the body and mind and can cause genuine changes in mind-set. An individual on drugs might be strangely discouraged or restless or more lively and euphoric than expected for no undeniable explanation.

Physical Indications of Drug Misuse

Social changes are significant indications of drug misuse. However, they can likewise be covered up somewhat. A few people manhandling drugs are genuinely adept at concealing the progressions that are happening, concealing their lackluster showing at school, professing to be locked in with family, or retaining data about their budgetary issues. The physical admonition indications of drug misuse are progressively hard to stow away, be that as it may. While various sorts of drugs cause direct physical side effects, some are basic with drug misuse, including:

- Changes in resting propensities, including dozing more or dozing less
- Eyes that are red or watery, or understudies that are excessively huge or excessively little
- Poor coordination, bumbling when strolling

- Slurred discourse, or making statements that are difficult to comprehend or don't bode well
- Tremors or shaking in any piece of the body
- A tenacious hack
- A runny nose
- Poor physical cleanliness
- Changes in dietary patterns, with either weight reduction or weight gain
- Pallor, flushing, or puffiness in the face
- Any strange scents on the dress, on the body, or the breath

Impacts of Regularly Mishandled Drugs

A considerable lot of indications of drug misuse are fundamental to a wide range of drugs. However, there are likewise some increasingly explicit side effects brought about by explicit drugs and substances. There are noticeable signs that can show an individual is manhandling drugs, yet also that they are mishandling at least one specific kind of drug. This is critical to comprehend because while all drug misuse is hurtful, a few substances can be more harmful than others and may require more squeezing mediation and treatment. A portion of the indications of maltreatment of necessary substances include:

Maryjane. Utilization of cannabis causes red eyes, a lustrous, clear gaze, happiness, and wrong chuckling, talking excessively noisy, detachment and absence of inspiration or enthusiasm for exercises, and weight changes.

Narcotics. Narcotics incorporate heroin and solution narcotic painkillers like OxyContin, hydrocodone, Vicodin, Percocet, Demerol, and others. These drugs cause the understudies to contract even in great lighting, loss of craving, unreasonable resting, spewing, hacking, sweating, jerks, and wheezing. Somebody utilizing heroin is probably going to have needle blemishes on the arms or feet.

Energizers. Energizers are drugs that expand the focal sensory system's movement and incorporate remedies like amphetamine and methamphetamine, just as cocaine, split, and gem meth, a solidified type of methamphetamine. Energizers cause happiness, expanded vitality, sharpness and less rest, diminished craving, weight reduction, dry mouth, peevishness, and uneasiness. Somebody on energizers might be hyper, conversational, and bright, and afterward, out of nowhere, discouraged.

Depressants. Depressants are tranquilizers that cause unwinding and languor. Remedy narcotics are utilized to treat a sleeping disorder and uneasiness. They incorporate barbiturates, sedatives, and benzodiazepines. These drugs cause lethargy, poor coordination, misguided thinking, slurred discourse, inconvenience concentrating, and different signs like being smashed.

Psychedelic drugs. These are drugs that cause fantasies and incorporate LSD, peyote, mushrooms, PCP, or heavenly attendant residue. Notwithstanding pipedreams, they cause expanded understudies, disarray, and slurred discourse, and neurosis, state of mind swings, separation, hostility, and distraction with specific things.

Inhalants. Inhalants are family unit synthetics that can be breathed to deliver a high, similar to pastes, pressurized canned products, and paints.

They mess memory up, rashes around the mouth or nose, runny nose, vision issues, cerebral pains, laziness, uneasiness, sickness, poor control of muscles, and changes in hunger.

Signs and Manifestations of Drug Addiction

The indications of drug misuse should be paid attention to because abuse of substances can cause unsafe symptoms, long-haul wellbeing results, addiction, and possibly deadly overdoses. Not all individuals who misuse drugs will get dependent on those substances, yet any drug abuse puts somebody in danger of addiction. Addiction to a drug causes a significant number of indistinguishable signs from drug misuse. However, there are additionally clear signs that an individual has gone too far from manhandling to being dependent, including:

- Building up resistance and requiring more noteworthy amounts of a drug to get a similar high or experience
- Utilizing a substance to maintain a strategic distance from or stop withdrawal side effects
- Never again having power overutilization of a drug; attempting to stop or utilize less yet flopping again and again
- Proceeding to utilize substances despite the damage it causes
- Everything rotates around getting a more significant amount of the drug

Getting Treatment for Drug Use or Addiction

It is a typical misguided judgment that somebody needs to wind up in a sorry situation before they can benefit from outside assistance. Sitting tight for drug maltreatment to form into addiction is risky.

On the off chance that you or somebody you care about is abusing drugs, get professional assistance as quickly as time permits. Somebody who is mishandling drugs can profit by time spent in a private treatment office where they can be assessed by addiction and emotional wellbeing authorities, get individualized treatment designs, and commit their time and vitality to show signs of improvement.

Treatment for substance use and addiction may include drugs now and again, yet social treatment is the spine. This treatment shows individuals how to perceive their negative considerations and practices, transform them, and utilize reliable procedures to adapt to negative feelings and abstain from utilizing substances later on. Treatment may likewise incorporate generally speaking wellbeing and elective treatment programs including nourishment, work out reflection, craft, or music treatment, and that's only the tip of the iceberg.

Drug misuse is harming people, their physical and psychological wellbeing, their fates, and their associations with families and friends and family. The indications of drug misuse can be covered up somewhat, yet on the off chance that you presume somebody you care about is utilizing, don't spare a moment to offer assistance and request that others step in intending to get the necessary treatment.

Chapter 2
Diagnosing the Type of Drug Addiction

A great many individuals required treatment for drug or alcohol use issues.

Addiction is a very much investigated field, with various treatment roads accessible for the individuals prepared to request the assist they require and need to have a more beneficial existence.

However, it likewise implies that treatment alternatives can feel overpowering from the start.

How would I realize I have an addiction?

The expression "addiction" isn't utilized any longer with regards to getting a conclusion. In the latest release, Symptomatic and Measurable Manual of

Mental Issue, drug and alcohol addiction is designated "use issue." The three most common side effects of a utilization issue include requiring a more significant amount of the substance after some time to accomplish a similar impact, encountering withdrawal indications when halting use, and not stopping in any event when you know there is a significant issue.

Use issues can go from gentle to severe, contingent upon the number of side effects you have. These manifestations include:

- Being unequipped for constraining drug or alcohol use.
- Making ineffective endeavors to abridge use.
- Spending much time utilizing or acquiring the substance.
- Experiencing longings to utilize.
- Falling behind in work, school, or family duties because of utilization.
- Continuing utilize in any event, when mindful of the issues it causes.

- Abandoning previous interests or leisure activities to take part being used.
- Drinking alcohol or utilizing drugs in dangerous circumstances, for example, driving.
- Requiring a more significant amount of the substance to accomplish a similar impact.

What ought to be my initial move towards recuperation?

Requesting help gives you the most obvious opportunity to change the example of addiction. Going only once in a while works, and confining will just set you up for backslide.

Getting help can look like conversing with your primary care physician, psychological wellbeing proficient, or a friend or family member.

You can likewise enroll the help of outsiders by going to a care group, for example, Alcoholics Mysterious, and requesting nearby proposals. Addiction is regular, so never be quiet for dread that you, despite everything, stun your primary care physician or instructor. Their main responsibility is to assist you with making that next stride.

Do I have to see a specialist or emotional wellbeing proficient?

Indeed. They will regard your privacy, so you should not hesitate to share all data about your utilization examples. A specialist or psychological wellbeing proficient can assess you to decide if you meet the utilization issue criteria. Drinking and drug use can cause genuine harm to your body, so it's essential to get looked at by a specialist. The person in question will direct a physical test and other essential tests. At the point when you go to your arrangement, share with your primary care physician any side effects you've encountered, your propensities for use, and other significant distressing life occasions that have happened as of late. The more data you can give them, the better consideration you will get.

How might I find support for a friend or family member with an addiction?

To start with, comprehend that recovery requires an ability to change. In any case, that doesn't mean you need to hold up until things hit absolute bottom to move toward your adored one about their unsafe conduct. In case you're thinking about arranging an intercession or moving toward your cherished one about the addiction, consistently talk with an expert first about how to keep away from hurt. They may suggest that they be in the stay with you to have the troublesome discussions. If your adored one isn't prepared to change, self-improvement gatherings like Al-Anon likewise can offer passionate help and direction for you and your family.

What are the attributes of an astounding treatment program?

For drug and alcohol use issues, there is an assortment of treatment choices. How would you realize which is best for you? An excellent treatment program will:

- Offer you detoxification support.
- Address all the individual's needs that the addiction impacts.
- Offer you directing and conduct support.
- Consider prescription as an alternative.
- Evaluate you for other emotional wellness concerns.
- Educate you about solid adapting abilities and propensities.
- Provide follow-up administrations to forestall future use.

What will happen once I choose to look for treatment?

There are three significant segments to stopping drug and alcohol use. The first is detoxification, where an individual swears off utilizing with the goal that the substance can leave their body. The drug is regularly endorsed during this phase to diminish the force of side effects. The subsequent advance includes looking for treatment, which may incorporate extra meds, advising, and assessing other emotional wellness issues. Treatment happens in outpatient or inpatient programs. The shame joined to addiction can dissuade numerous individuals from looking for treatment; however, it is significant that you get the assistance you need. At last, you should discover support for the long haul to forestall backsliding on the substance.

Would it be a good idea for me to pick inpatient or outpatient treatment?

Contingent upon the assets accessible, what your medical coverage is eager to cover, the force of the confusion, and the kind of utilization issue, emotional wellness experts may propose inpatient or outpatient social wellbeing treatment.

Inpatient treatment – Inpatient programs are daily offices that give lodging, clinical consideration, and treatment for those with severe addictions.

Over a portion of individuals who get treatment for drug or alcohol use issues takes an interest in inpatient treatment.

Inpatient treatment programs incorporate momentary detox habitats, long haul programs which last anyplace from half a month to a year, or recuperation programs which give lodging to connect the progress to independent living.

Long haul programs are frequently suggested for those with an extra psychological instability finding who require additional help or people with a criminal history.

Outpatient treatment – Outpatient treatment can run from an individual treatment meeting once per week to increasingly severe day programs that offer individual and gathering treatment, psych educational classes, and different exercises. The distinctive factor is that outpatient treatment isn't every minute of every day and doesn't generally give nearby clinical consideration. People may progress to outpatient treatment from detox focuses or more extended inpatient treatment programs.

What sorts of treatment have been demonstrated to work?

Numerous kinds of treatment and various social intercessions have demonstrated viability in treating addiction.

The most commonly utilized treatment is subjective social treatment, which helps individuals assess and address negative idea examples and practices that lead to addiction.

Conduct treatment; for example, REBT can give uplifting feedback systems that energize proceeding with balance. Gathering treatment has additionally demonstrated compelling when it happens simultaneously with precise guiding. Multidimensional family treatment analyzes how improving the working of a family framework can decrease drug and alcohol misuse triggers.

An undeniably traditional instrument utilized in addiction treatment is called a persuasive meeting (otherwise called MI).

Utilized by specialists, advisors, and other wellbeing experts, inspirational talking is a conversational method that helps individuals survey their availability to stop the conduct and look for treatment.

As opposed to attempting to persuade an individual to change a propensity, MI recognizes that there are beneficial things and awful things about utilizing drugs and alcohol and not utilizing them. This enables a person to be progressively alright, moving towards rolling out a lasting improvement.

Will I be endorsed prescription?

Prescription alone can't fix drug and alcohol use issues; however, it can demonstrate viability amazingly in lessening the manifestations of withdrawal and the chance of backslide. Pharmacotherapy can likewise help lessen the indications of other psychological sicknesses, for example, nervousness and misery that advance drug and alcohol use. Meds are ordinarily endorsed for those dependent on narcotics (counting solutions drugs and heroin) and alcohol.

Narcotic use drugs incorporate methadone, buprenorphine, and naltrexone.

Methadone and buprenorphine work to decrease desires and the force of withdrawal manifestations, and naltrexone keeps narcotics from having their typical impact on the cerebrum.

While these prescriptions don't fix the addiction, they help set up a person for treatment and assessing what changes can assist them with looking after balance. Alcohol use prescriptions incorporate naltrexone, acamprosate, and disulfiram.

Acamprosate decreases side effects of withdrawal, such as melancholy or tension sentiments, along these lines diminishing backslide's opportunity. Disulfiram (otherwise called Antabuse) produces troublesome physical responses when somebody drinks alcohol, for example, sickness and facial re

What way of life changes would I be able to make to forestall backslide?

When you leave a treatment program, you may find that your old triggers will be looking out for the doorstep when you return home. It's imperative to disclose to your loved ones that you're not kidding about recuperation.

Create connections that aren't founded on drinking or utilizing drugs. Know when and where care groups meet in your neighborhood. Keep up a good ways from individuals, spots, and occasions that advance old propensities. The vast majority with use issues experience backslide. While a backslide may be upsetting, it is no reason to surrender trust.

Carrying on with a more useful life can likewise lift your state of mind, give you vitality, and diminish the longings for alcohol or drugs. Getting a legitimate night's rest, practicing typically, and adapting to pressure viably can have a tremendous effect. Unwinding methods, for example, care and yoga, can likewise demonstrate instrumental in recovery.

Will alcohol and drug use issues honestly be dealt with?

Indeed! Know in any case, that detox is only the initial step. Addiction is ceaseless, implying that it is a long-lasting test. Unpleasant occasions, uneasiness, discouragement, and different variables can trigger a backslide, so the vast majority need extended haul support for their choice to stop. Perhaps you'll generally pine for the substance, or possibly you won't. However, you can control what goes into your

There are various administrations accessible to help an individual encountering substance reliance. It is hard to figure out which kind of treatment is ideal, as this is profoundly subject to the individual's necessities requiring the administration.

Various medicines focus on different results, regardless of whether it's all out forbearance or decrease of substance use to a more secure and less unsafe level.

Alternatives incorporate individual advising, bunch treatment, and drug to facilitate the side effects of withdrawal.

Not every person finishes a treatment program the first or even second time; however, this doesn't mean an individual can't look for help once more. A few people discover they have to investigate various diverse treatment alternatives before finding what works for them.

Admission and evaluation for substance reliance

In Victoria, an individual who needs support for a substance issue will be given a screening and evaluation administration to decide the most practical help for their requirements. The vast majority get to government-financed treatment benefits through a helpline or the admission and appraisal supplier in their general vicinity.

There are additional entrance and referral game plans for Native and Torres Waterway Islander people groups, youngsters, measurable customers, and individuals treated under the Extreme Substance Reliance Treatment Act 2010.

The admission and evaluation process, embraced by the Division of Wellbeing and Human Administrations, guarantees a reliable procedure across administrations and lessens individuals' requirement to rehash their story.

The admission procedure empowers admission and appraisal administrations to:

- Recognize how severe the individual's substance use is and how it is affecting their life
- Recognize high-hazard individuals who will require quick help
- Recognize individuals who may require additional help
- Become familiar with alcohol and other drug issues to improve bolster administrations.

With the individual's consent, the admission procedure's outcomes might be shared among medicinal services suppliers to help treatment.

Beginning treatment plan

The alcohol and different drugs professional who gives the appraisal builds up an underlying treatment plan with the customer. The underlying treatment plan incorporates data gathered from the screening and appraisal process, just as its distinguished treatment needs and the customer's inclinations. The arrangement is remembered for a bundle of referral data gave by admission and evaluation administrations to treatment specialist co-ops.

Brief mediation for substance reliance

Fast mediation implies endeavoring to treat individuals in the last phases of their substance use before creating genuine substance-related issues. It depends on the hypothesis that individuals can deal with their substance use and related issues on the off chance that they are given the relevant data or other mediation at the perfect time.

These mediation meetings may incorporate an evaluation of the individual's substance use and arrangement of a self-improvement manual or other data. Brief intercession has been utilized effectively with individuals who smoke cigarettes and drink alcohol vigorously.

Directing choices for substance reliance

An individual can get individual or gathering advising as an outpatient or a significant aspect of inpatient treatment. The various models of guiding may include:

- The Egan model – the individual chooses which issues are significant and the ideal approaches to address them, with the advisor as a 'sounding board.'

- Inspirational talking – the individual is urged to decrease their degree of drug use by investigating the outcomes of their addiction and the advantages of social change. They are assuming liability for their conduct, and dynamic causes them to see their capacity to make changes throughout their lives.

- Psychological conduct treatment (CBT) – the individual is assisted with beating nonsensical considerations. The hypothesis plans to change how individuals consider their conduct.

- The framework hypothesis –advising that puts an individual regarding family, social, social, and different conditions in which they live. The hypothesis suggests that adjustment in one territory makes a change in different territories.

Substance detoxification (withdrawal) programs

Detoxification ('detox'), or withdrawal, is a program to free the individual's assemblage of lethal substance levels. An individual reliant on a substance may experience the ill effects of withdrawal side effects when they quit utilizing it.

Withdrawal from specific substances– alcohol and minor sedatives (benzodiazepines) – can be hazardous in outrageous conditions. In this way, a clinical evaluation should be considered before an individual pulls back from a substance. Clinical withdrawal implies utilizing other prescriptions to facilitate the side effects of withdrawal. This can be brought out either in a medical clinic or through a substance withdrawal administration.

Common withdrawal side effects can include:

- Sleep deprivation
- Queasiness
- Shaking
- Perspiring
- Extreme lethargies or demise, in exceptionally uncommon cases.

Mischief decrease when breaking substance reliance

Mischief decrease perceives that numerous individuals typically use substances of some sort, for example, alcohol. As opposed to pointing solely for forbearance, the idea of mischief decrease focuses on diminishing drug use or changing drug use conduct, so it is less hurtful to the individual utilizing the substance.

A model is the needle trade program, which is intended to lessen the frequency of HIV and other blood-borne infections that can be gone through individuals utilizing intravenous drugs and sharing needles. For some individuals, diminishing substance use is a more sensible objective than stopping through and through.

Pharmacotherapy and medicine to treat substance reliance

In some cases, an endorsed prescription is utilized to supplant the substance an individual is attempting to quit utilizing. This is called substitution pharmacotherapy. For instance, methadone is here and there endorsed for heroin reliance (addiction).

Methadone is an engineered drug that is assumed in the position of heroin. Like heroin, methadone has a place with the sedative family. While it doesn't give the equivalent 'high' as heroin, it facilitates the withdrawal indications. Methadone works for longer than heroin, so it should be taken once day by day rather than at regular intervals. While substitution pharmacotherapy may not be appropriate for everybody, and there are no pharmacotherapies accessible for all substances, it has various advantages.

Contingent upon the substance an individual is utilizing, a portion of these advantages can include:

- A facilitating of withdrawal manifestations, which permits the individual to work in everyday life
- The individual is never again taking a substance that is made in a 'lawn lab' with no quality control or information on its immaculateness
- The individual is never again utilizing a substance in unsafe sums or utilizing a conceivably risky strategy, for example, infusing
- They are furnishing an individual with the opportunity to address their life issues without stressing over discovering enough cash every day, getting the substance, utilizing it.

A few instances of pharmacotherapies for various substances include:

- Alcohol – acamprosate (Campral), disulfiram (Antabuse), naltrexone (Revia)

- Narcotics, (for example, heroin) – buprenorphine (Subutex, Suboxone), methadone, naltrexone (Revia)
- Tobacco – nicotine substitution treatments (NRT, for example, patches, gum and inhalers, bupropion (Zyban), clonidine, nortriptyline.

Backslide avoidance during substance reliance treatment

Individuals experiencing substance reliance treatment need significant help to make adequate progress to a substance way of life. There are different help programs accessible, such as enabling the individual to discover business or lodging.

Network support for substance reliance

An individual with a substance issue can pick up bits of knowledge into their substance use by conversing with other people who have been in a comparable circumstance.

A significant number of these gatherings can likewise offer help administrations.

Likewise, there are 'restorative networks,' which empower self-awareness through the comprehension and care of others in the network. An individual may join a strong network for a considerable length of time or years.

Chapter 3
Approaches towards Treatment & Principles of Prevention

Treatment Approaches for Drug Addiction

Drug addiction is a constant ailment described by urgent, or wild, drug chasing and use notwithstanding destructive results and changes in the cerebrum, which can be dependable. These adjustments in the cerebrum can prompt the destructive practices found in individuals who use drugs. Drug addiction is additionally a backsliding sickness. Backslide is the arrival of drug use after an endeavor to stop.

The way to drug addiction starts with the intentional demonstration of consuming medications. Be that as it may, after some time, an individual's capacity to decide not to do so becomes traded off. Looking for and taking the drug gets enthusiastic.

This is generally because of the impacts of long haul drug introduction on cerebrum work. Addiction influences portions of the mind associated with remuneration and inspiration, learning and memory, and power over conduct. Addiction is a disorder that influences both the mind and conduct.

Can drug addiction be dealt with?

Indeed, yet it's not necessary. Since addiction is a constant infection, individuals can't just quit utilizing drugs for a couple of days and be relieved. Most patients need long haul or rehashed care to quit utilizing totally and recoup their lives. Addiction treatment must assistance the individual do the accompanying:

- Quit utilizing drugs
- Stay without drug
- Be beneficial in the family, grinding away, and in the public eye

Standards of Successful Treatment

In light of logical research since the mid-1970s, the accompanying vital standards should shape the premise of any viable treatment program:

- Addiction is a complex yet treatable illness that influences cerebrum capacity and conduct.
- No single treatment is directly for everybody.
- Individuals need to have fast access to treatment.
- Successful treatment tends to the entirety of the patient's needs, not merely their drug use.
- Remaining in treatment long enough is basic.
- Advising and other social treatments are the most typically utilized types of treatment.
- Drugs are frequently a significant piece of treatment, particularly when joined with conduct treatments.
- Treatment plans must be surveyed regularly and altered to fit the patient's evolving needs.
- Treatment should address another potential mental issue.

- Restoratively helped detoxification is just the principal phase of treatment.
- Treatment shouldn't be willful to be compelling.
- Drug use during treatment must be observed consistently.

Treatment projects should test patients for HIV/Helps, hepatitis B and C, tuberculosis, and different irresistible sicknesses, just as instruct them about advances they can take to diminish their danger of these diseases.

What are medications for drug addiction?

Numerous alternatives have been effective in treating drug addiction, including:

- Social guiding
- Drugs
- Clinical gadgets and applications used to treat withdrawal side effects or convey aptitudes preparing

- Assessment and treatment for co-happening emotional wellbeing issues, for example, discouragement and nervousness
- Long haul follow-up to forestall backslide

Scope of care with a customized treatment program and follow-up choices can be vital to progress. Treatment ought to incorporate both clinical and emotional wellness benefits varying. Follow-up care may incorporate network or family-based recuperation emotionally supportive networks.

How are meds and gadgets utilized in drug addiction treatment?

Meds and gadgets can be utilized to oversee withdrawal side effects, forestall backslide, and treat co-happening conditions.

Withdrawal. Meds and gadgets can help stifle withdrawal manifestations during detoxification. Detoxification isn't in itself "treatment," however, just the initial phase all the while. Patients who don't get any further treatment after detoxification typically continue their drug use. One investigation of treatment offices found that drugs were utilized in just about 80 percent of detoxifications (SAMHSA, 2014). In November 2017, the Nourishment and Drug Organization (FDA) allowed another sign to an electronic incitement gadget, NSS-2 Extension, to diminish narcotic withdrawal indications. This gadget is set behind the ear and sends electrical heartbeats to invigorate specific cerebrum nerves. Additionally, in May 2018, the FDA affirmed lofexidine, a non-narcotic medication intended to lessen narcotic withdrawal side effects.

Backslide avoidance. Patients can utilize prescriptions to enable re-to to build up ordinary mind capacity and decline desires. Drugs are accessible to treat narcotic (heroin, remedy torment relievers), tobacco (nicotine), and alcohol addiction. Researchers are creating different prescriptions to treat energizer (cocaine, methamphetamine) and cannabis (Maryjane) addiction. Individuals who utilize more than one drug, which is exceptionally standard, need treatment for all the substances they use.

Narcotics: Methadone (Dolophine®, Methadose®), buprenorphine (Suboxone®, Subutex®, Probuphine®, Sublocade™), and naltrexone (Vivitrol®) are utilized to treat narcotic addiction.

Following up on indistinguishable focuses on the mind from heroin and morphine, methadone and buprenorphine stifle withdrawal side effects and assuage yearnings.

Naltrexone obstructs the impacts of narcotics at their receptor locales in mind and should be utilized distinctly in patients who have just been detoxified. All prescriptions assist patients with diminishing drug chasing and related criminal conduct and assist them with getting progressively open to social medicines.

A NIDA study found that once treatment is started, both a buprenorphine/naloxone mix and an all-encompassing discharge naltrexone plan are comparatively successful in treating narcotic addiction. Since full detoxification is essential for treatment with naloxone, starting treatment among dynamic clients was troublesome; however, once detoxification was finished, the two prescriptions had comparable adequacy.

Tobacco: Nicotine substitution treatments have a few structures, including the fix, splash, gum, and capsules. These items are accessible over the counter. The U.S. Nourishment and Drug Organization (FDA) has endorsed two physicians endorsed meds for nicotine addiction: bupropion (Zyban®) and varenicline (Chantix®). They work diversely in mind; however, both assistance forestalls backslide in individuals attempting to stop. The prescriptions are increasingly powerful when joined with conduct medications, for example, gathering and individual treatment just as phone quitlines.

Alcohol: Three drugs have been FDA-affirmed for treating alcohol addiction, and a fourth, topiramate, has indicated a guarantee in clinical preliminaries (enormous scope concentrates with individuals). The three endorsed meds are as per the following:

Naltrexone squares narcotic receptors associated with the compensating impacts of drinking and in the desire for alcohol. It diminishes backslide to substantial drinking and is profoundly viable in individual patients. Hereditary contrasts may influence how well the drug functions in specific patients.

Acamprosate (Campral®) may diminish enduring withdrawal symptoms, for example, a sleeping disorder, uneasiness, eagerness, and dysphoria (for the most part feeling unwell or troubled).

It might be progressively powerful in patients with extreme addiction.

Disulfiram (Antabuse®) meddles with the breakdown of alcohol.

Acetaldehyde develops in the body, prompting horrendous responses that incorporate flushing (warmth and redness in the face), sickness, and irregular heartbeat if the patient beverages alcohol. Consistency (accepting the drug as recommended) can be an issue, yet it might help patients who are exceptionally energetic to stop drinking.

Co-occurring conditions: Different meds are accessible to treat conceivable psychological wellness conditions, for example, gloom or tension that might be adding to the individual's addiction.

Realistic of segments of far-reaching drug addiction treatment with an out and inward circle.

The outer circle records professional administrations, psychological wellness administrations, clinical administrations, instructive administrations, HIV/Helps administrations, lawful administrations, and family benefits.

The internal circle records evaluation, proof-based treatment, substance use observed, clinical and cased the board, recuperation bolster programs and proceeding with care. The subtitle is the best treatment program to give a mix of treatments and others.

How are conduct treatments used to treat drug addiction?

Conduct treatments help patients:

- Change their perspectives and practices identified with drug use
- Increment solid fundamental abilities

- Endure with different types of treatment, for example, medicine

Patients can get treatment in a wide range of settings with different methodologies.

Outpatient social treatment incorporates a wide assortment of projects for patients who visit a wellbeing instructor on a standard timetable. The vast majority of the projects include individual or gathering drug directing, or both.

These projects typically offer types of social treatment, for example, social psychological treatment, which enables patients to perceive, keep away from, and adapt to the circumstances where they are well on the way to utilize drugs multidimensional family treatment—produced for young people with drug misuse issues just as their families—which tends to a scope of effects on their drug misuse designs and is intended to improve in the general family working inspirational talking, which benefits as much as possible from individuals' status to change their conduct and enter persuasive treatment motivators (a possibility the board), which utilizes uplifting feedback to empower forbearance from drugs

In some cases, treatment escalated from the outset, where patients go to numerous outpatient meetings every week. In the wake of finishing severe treatment, patients progress to standard outpatient treatment, which meets less frequently and fewer hours out of each week to help continue their healing. In September 2017, the FDA promoted the main portable application, reSET®, to treat substance use issues. This application is planned to be utilized with outpatient treatment to treat alcohol, cocaine, pot, and energizer substance use issue. In December 2018, the FDA cleared a portable clinical application, reSET®, to help treat the narcotic use issue. This application is a remedy for the intellectual, social treatment and should incorporate buprenorphine and the executives' possibility. Peruse increasingly about reSET® right now Discharge.

Inpatient or private treatment can likewise be extremely successful, particularly for those with increasingly serious issues (counting co-happening issue).

Authorized private treatment offices offer 24-hour organized and escalated care, including safe lodging and clinical consideration. Private treatment offices may utilize an assortment of remedial methodologies, and they are by and large planned for helping the patient live without drug, wrongdoing free way of life after treatment. Instances of private treatment settings include:

Remedial people group, which are profoundly organized projects in which patients stay at a habitation, ordinarily for 6 to a year.

The whole network, including treatment staff and those in healing, go about as critical specialists of progress, affecting the patient's mentalities, comprehension, and practices related to drug use. Peruse progressively about remedial networks in the Restorative People group Exploration Report at https://www.drugabuse.gov/productions/look into reports/helpful networks.

Shorter-term private treatment, which commonly centers on detoxification just as giving beginning serious guiding and groundwork for treatment in a network-based setting.

Recuperation lodging gives managed, momentary lodging for patients, frequently following different sorts of inpatient or private treatment. Recuperation lodging can help individuals progress to an autonomous life—for instance, helping them figure out how to oversee funds or look for work, just as interfacing them to help the network's benefits.

Is treatment diverse for criminal equity populaces?

Analytical research since the mid-1970s shows that drug misuse treatment can help many drug-utilizing guilty parties change their perspectives, convictions, and practices towards drug misuse; maintain a strategic distance from backsliding, and effectively expel themselves from an existence of substance misuse and wrongdoing.

A significant number of treating drug addiction standards are comparable for individuals inside the criminal equity framework for those in everybody. Be that as it may, numerous guilty parties don't approach the kinds of administrations they need. Treatment that is of low quality or isn't appropriate to wrongdoers' requirements may not be powerful at diminishing drug use and criminal conduct. Notwithstanding the general standards of treatment, a few contemplations explicit to guilty parties incorporate the accompanying.

Treatment should incorporate the advancement of explicit intellectual abilities to enable the guilty party to alter perspectives and convictions that lead to drug misuse and wrongdoing, for example, feeling qualified for having things in one's particular manner or not understanding the outcomes of one's conduct. This incorporates aptitudes identified with intuition, getting, learning, and recollecting.

Treatment arranging ought to incorporate custom-made administrations inside the restorative office to progress to network-based treatment after discharge. Continuous coordination between treatment suppliers and courts or parole and post-trial supervisors is significant intending to the complex needs of guilty parties reemerging society.

Difficulties of Reemergence

Drug misuse changes the cerebrum's capacity, and numerous things can "trigger" drug yearnings inside the mind. It's fundamental for those in treatment, particularly those treated at an inpatient office or jail, to figure out how to perceive, stay away from, and adapt to triggers they are probably going to be presented to after treatment.

What number of individuals get treatment for drug addiction?

As indicated by SAMHSA's National Review on Drug Use and Wellbeing, 22.5 million individuals (8.5 percent of the U.S. populace) matured 12 or more established required treatment for an illicit* drug or alcohol use issue in 2014. Just 4.2 million (18.5 percent of the individuals who required treatment) got any substance use treatment around the same time. Of these, about 2.6 million individuals got treatment at strength treatment programs (CBHSQ,

2015). The term "unlawful" alludes to using illicit drugs, including marijuana as per government law, and abuse of doctor prescribed prescriptions.

Focuses on Recall

Drug addiction can be dealt with, yet it's not straightforward. Addiction treatment must assistance the individual do the accompanying:

- Quit utilizing drugs
- Stay sans drug
- Be gainful in the family, grinding away, and in the public arena

Effective treatment has a few stages:

- Detoxification
- Conduct advising
- Prescription (for narcotic, tobacco, or alcohol addiction)
- Assessment and treatment for co-happening emotional wellness issues, for example, sadness and nervousness
- Long haul follow-up to forestall backslide

Meds and gadgets can be utilized to oversee withdrawal indications, forestall backslide, and treat co-happening conditions. Conduct treatments help patients:

- Adjust their perspectives and practices identified with drug use
- Increment solid fundamental abilities
- Persevere with different types of treatment, for example, prescription

Individuals inside the criminal equity framework may require different treatment administrations to treat drug use issue viably. In any case, numerous wrongdoers don't approach the sorts of administrations they need.

The standards recorded beneath are the aftereffect of long haul look into concentrates on the birthplaces of drug misuse practices and the typical components of effective avoidance programs.

These standards were created to help avoidance professionals utilize the consequences of anticipation research to address drug use among kids, teenagers, and youthful grown-ups in networks the nation over.

Guardians, teachers, and network pioneers can utilize these standards to help direct their reasoning, arranging, determination, and conveyance of drug misuse counteraction programs at the network level.

Avoidance programs are commonly intended for use in a specific setting, for example, at home, at school, or inside the network. However, it can be adjusted for use in a few settings.

What's more, programs are additionally planned because of the target group: for everybody in the populace, those at more serious hazard, and those effects associated with drugs or other issue practices. A few projects can be intended for more than one crowd.

NIDA's anticipation investigates program centers around dangers for drug misuse and other issues that happen through a kid's improvement, from pregnancy through youthful adulthood. Research financed by NIDA and other Governments look into associations, for example, the National Organization of Psychological wellbeing and the Places for Sickness Control and Counteraction—shows that early mediation can forestall numerous youthful hazard practices.

Guideline 1 - Avoidance projects should upgrade defensive factors and decrease chance variables (Hawkins et al. 2002). The danger of turning into a drug abuser includes the relationship among the number and sort of hazard factors (e.g., degenerate perspectives and practices) and defensive elements (e.g., parental help) (Wills et al. 1996).

The potential effect of explicit hazard and defensive elements changes with age. For instance, chance factors inside the family have a more prominent effect on a more youthful kid, while the relationship with drug-manhandling friends might be an increasingly influential hazard factor for a pre-adult (Gerstein and Green 1993; Dishion et al. 1999).

Early intercession with hazard factors (e.g., violent conduct and inadequate restraint) regularly has a more remarkable effect than later mediation by changing a youngster's life way (direction) away from issues and toward positive practices (Ialongo et al. 2001; Hawkins et al. 2008).

While chance and defensive elements can influence individuals, these elements can have an alternate impact contingent upon an individual's age, sexual orientation, ethnicity, culture, and condition (Beauvais et al. 1996; Moon et al. 1999).

Guideline 2 - Avoidance projects should address all types of drug misuse, alone or in a blend, including the underage utilization of legitimate drugs (e.g., tobacco or alcohol); the utilization of unlawful drugs (e.g., weed or heroin); and the wrong utilization of lawfully acquired substances (e.g., inhalants), doctor-prescribed meds, or over-the-counter drugs (Johnston et al. 2002).

Guideline 3 - Avoidance projects should address drug misuse issues in the nearby network, target modifiable hazard factors, and fortify recognized defensive elements (Hawkins et al. 2002).

Guideline 4 - Counteraction projects ought to be custom-fitted to deliver dangers explicit to populace or crowd attributes, for example, age, sexual orientation, and ethnicity, to improve program viability (Oetting et al. 1997; Olds et al. 1998; Fisher et al. 2007; Brody et al. 2008).

Guideline 5 - Family-based anticipation projects should upgrade family holding and connections and incorporate child-rearing abilities; practice in creating, talking about, and authorizing family strategies on substance misuse; and preparing in drug instruction and data (Ashery et al. 1998). Family holding is the bedrock of the connection between guardians and youngsters. Holding can be fortified by preparing for kids' parent steadiness, parent-youngster correspondence, and parental contribution (Kosterman et al. 1997; Spoth et al. 2004).

Parental observing and supervision are necessary for drug misuse counteraction. These abilities can be upgraded with preparing on rule-setting, observing exercises, acclaiming proper conduct, and moderate, predictable control that implements characterized family governs (Kosterman et al. 2001).

Drug training and data for guardians or parental figures fortifies what youngsters are finding out about the destructive impacts of drugs and opens open doors for family conversations about the maltreatment of legitimate and illicit substances (Bauman et al. 2001). Brief, family-engaged mediations for everybody can emphatically change explicit child-rearing conduct that can diminish later dangers of drug misuse (Spoth et al. 2002b).

Guideline 6 - Counteraction projects can be intended to mediate as right on time as outset to address hazard factors for drug misuse, for example, violent conduct, poor social abilities, and scholastic troubles (Webster-Stratton 1998; Olds et al. 1998; Webster-Stratton et al. 2001; Fisher et al. 2007).

Guideline 7 - Avoidance programs for primary younger students should target improving scholarly and social-enthusiastic figuring out how to address hazard factors for drug misuse, for example, early hostility, scholastic disappointment, and school dropout. Training should concentrate on the accompanying abilities (Lead Issues Avoidance Exploration Gathering 2002; Ialongo et al. 2001; Riggs et al. 2006; Kellam et al. 2008; Beets et al. 2009):

- Restraint
- Passionate mindfulness
- Correspondence
- Social critical thinking and
- Academic help, particularly in perusing

Guideline 8 - Counteraction programs for center or middle school and secondary school understudies should expand academic and social ability with the accompanying aptitudes (Botvin et al. 1995; Scheier et al. 1999; Eisen et al. 2003; Ellickson et al. 2003; Haggerty et al. 2007): study propensities and scholastic help

- Correspondence
- Peer connections
- Self-viability and emphatics
- Drug opposition aptitudes

- Fortification of hostile to drug mentalities and
- Fortifying of individual duties against drug misuse

Guideline 9 - Anticipation programs focused on overall communities at critical progress focuses, for example, the change to center school, can create beneficial impacts even among high-hazard families and youngsters. Such mediations don't single out hazard populaces and, along these lines, diminish naming and elevate attaching to class and network (Botvin et al. 1995; Dishion et al. 2002; Establishment of Medication 2009).

Guideline 10 - Network anticipation programs that consolidate at least two successful projects, for example, family-based and school-based projects, can be more viable than a solitary program alone (Battistich et al. 1997; Spoth et al. 2002c; Stormshak et al. 2005).

Guideline 11 - Network counteraction programs arriving at populaces in different settings—for instance, schools, clubs, religious associations, and the media—are best when they present steady, network-wide messages in each setting (Chou et al. 1998; Hawkins et al. 2009).

Guideline 12 - When people group adjust projects to coordinate their needs, network standards, or contrasting social prerequisites, they ought to hold center components of the first research-based mediation (Spoth et al. 2002b; Hawkins et al. 2009), which include:

- Structure (how the program is sorted out and developed)
- Content (the data, aptitudes, and methodologies of the program) and
- Conveyance (how the program is adjusted, executed, and assessed)

Guideline 13 - Anticipation projects ought to be a long haul with rehashed mediations (i.e., sponsor programs) to strengthen the first avoidance objectives. Research shows that the advantages of center school avoidance programs reduce without follow-up programs in secondary school (Botvin et al. 1995; Scheier et al. 1999).

Guideline 14 - Avoidance projects should incorporate educators preparing on great study hall the executives rehearses, such as remunerating suitable understudy conduct. Such systems encourage understudies' certain conduct, accomplishment, scholastic inspiration, and school holding (Ialongo et al. 2001; Kellam et al. 2008).

Guideline 15 - Counteraction programs are best when they utilize intelligent systems, for example, peer conversation gatherings and parent pretending, that take into account dynamic contribution in finding out about drug misuse and fortifying abilities (Botvin et al. 1995).

Guideline 16 - Exploration based counteraction projects can be financially savvy. Like prior research, ongoing examination shows that for every dollar to put resources into counteraction, investment funds of up to $10 in treatment for alcohol or other substance misuses can be seen.

Chapter 4
Types of Treatments and Therapies

Addictive clutters a gathering of disarranges that can cause physical and mental harm. Getting treatment is necessary for breaking the pattern of addiction. Be that as it may, as an interminable disorder, addiction is hard to treat and requires on-going consideration.

In the U.S., around 8.1 percent of the populace, or 21.7 million individuals, either require or routinely get treatment for substance use issues, as indicated by the National Overview on Drug Use and Wellbeing.

Initial steps

The initial step to recovery is recognizing the nearness of addiction and its consequences for daily life. The initial move towards recuperation recognizes that substance use has become an issue in the individual's life, upsetting a fantastic nature.

This can result from hindrance in school, work, social, recreational, or other significant capacity zones. When individuals perceive the negative effect of a substance on their lives, a broad scope of treatment choices is accessible.

An individual with an addictive issue expects access to treatment. For the vast majority, treatment may keep going for a fantastic remainder. They should refrain from the substance on a deep-rooted premise, which can be troublesome. Treatment plans for addictive scatter will frequently change to address the issues of the patient.

Treatment alternatives for addiction rely upon a few components, including the sort of addictive issue, the length and seriousness of utilization, and its impacts on the person.

A specialist will likewise treat or allude for treatment any physical complexities that have grown, such as liver illness in an individual with alcohol use issue or respiratory issues in individuals with an addiction to substances that have been smoked.

A few treatment choices are accessible, and the vast majority of encountering addiction will get a blend of approaches. None of the medications for addictive disarranges work for each individual.

Necessary mediations may include inpatient and outpatient programs, mental guiding, self-improvement gatherings, and medicine.

Detoxification

Detoxification is typically the initial phase in treatment. This includes clearing a substance from the body and constraining withdrawal responses. In 80 percent of cases, a treatment center will utilize meds to reduce withdrawal side effects, as per the Substance Misuse and Psychological wellbeing Administrations Organization (SAMHSA). If individuals are dependent on more than one substance, they will regularly require drugs to decrease their withdrawal side effects.

In 2017, an electronic gadget called the NSS-2 Extension opened up to diminish sedative withdrawal. The gadget sits behind the ear and emits electrical heartbeats to trigger specific nerves that may alleviate withdrawal indications.

- Advising and social treatments

- Treatment may be coordinated or a gathering meeting.
- This is the most well-known type of treatment following detoxification.

Treatment may happen on a coordinated, gathering, or family premise contingent upon the person's requirements. It usually is severe at the beginning of treatment, with the quantity of meetings step by step decreasing after some time as indications improve.

Various sorts of treatment include:

Subjective social treatment helps individuals with perceiving and change perspectives that have a relationship with substance use.

Multidimensional family treatment, intended to help improve family work around a pre-adult or high schooler with a substance-related turmoil

Persuasive talking, which expands a people readiness to change and make acclimations to practices

Inspirational motivators that support restraint through encouraging feedback

Guiding for addiction intends to assist individuals with changing practices and mentalities around utilizing a substance, reinforcing fundamental abilities, and supporting different medicines.

In 2017, the U.S. Nourishment and Drug Organization (FDA) affirmed the main ever-versatile application, reSET®, as successful for use close by outpatient the executives for cannabis, cocaine, alcohol, and energizer use issue.

A few treatment types for addictive clutters center on the hidden reason for the addictive issue, notwithstanding practices every day.

Recovery programs

Longer-term treatment programs for substance-related and addictive can be profoundly successful and commonly center on outstanding sans drug and continuing capacity inside social, expert, and family duties. Completely authorized private offices are accessible to structure a 24-hour care program, give a sheltered lodging condition, and supply any essential clinical intercessions or help.

A couple of sorts of the office can give a refreshing domain, including:

Transient private treatment: This spotlights detoxification and setting up a person for a more extended period inside a remedial network through concentrated advising.

Restorative people group: An individual looking for long haul treatment for extreme types of addictive issues would live in a living arrangement for somewhere in the range of 6 and a year with on-location staff and others in healing. The people group and staff fill crucial factors in healing from and changes in drug use perspectives and practices.

Recuperation lodging: This gives a regulated, momentary remain in lodging to assist individuals with connecting with obligations and adjust to another, free existence without on-going substance use. Recuperation lodging remembers guidance for taking care of funds and looking for employment, just as giving the association between an individual during the last phases of recovery and network bolster administrations.

Self-improvement gatherings

Gathering treatment and long haul recovery can assist an individual with a substance utilize clutter feel less disengaged. These may help the recuperating singular meet others with the equivalent addictive issue, which frequently supports inspiration and diminishes detachment sentiments. They can likewise fill in as a valuable wellspring of instruction, network, and data.

Models incorporate Alcoholics Mysterious (A.A.) and Opiates Unknown (N.A.).

Individuals battling different sorts of addiction can get answers concerning self-improvement gatherings in their locale either by a web search or by approaching a specialist or medical caretaker for data.

Prescriptions

An individual may take drug consistently while recouping from a substance-related turmoil and its related difficulties.

Be that as it may, individuals most usually use prescriptions during detoxification to oversee withdrawal side effects.

The medicine will change contingent upon the substance that the individual is dependent on.

Longer-term utilization of prescriptions assists with diminishing desires and forestall backslide, or arrival to utilizing the substance in the wake of having recouped from addiction. The drug isn't an independent treatment for addiction and ought to go with other administration strategies, for example, psychotherapy. Addiction to the accompanying substances requires explicit meds.

Alcohol

Individuals with alcohol use issue can take the accompanying meds to decrease longings and withdrawal indications, including:

Naltrexone: This forestalls the activity of narcotic receptors in the cerebrum that produce fulfilling and euphoric impacts when an individual expends alcohol and diminishes the danger of backsliding. While not compelling for all individuals in healing, it considerably affects forbearance in specific individuals.

Acamprosate, or Campral: This may lessen long haul withdrawal indications, including restlessness, nervousness, and a general sentiment of misery known as dysphoria. This has a progressively beneficial impact on individuals with extreme substance-related and addictive scatters.

Disulfiram, or Antabuse: This is a prescription that upsets the breakdown of alcohol, prompting antagonistic impacts including facial redness, feeling wiped out, and an unpredictable heartbeat should the individual in recuperation endeavor to devour alcohol. It goes about as an obstacle for individuals who have high inspiration levels toward recuperation.

Specialists and recovery authorities may recommend other prescriptions to address other conceivable emotional wellness conditions, including hopelessness and tension, that might be a reason or consequence of substance-related disarranges.

Individuals in treatment projects should likewise get testing for irresistible sicknesses that may have come about because of certain high-chance circumstances related to their addictive issues, such as HIV, hepatitis, and tuberculosis.

Takeaway

Substance-related scatters are persistent, complex illnesses that require delayed, concentrated treatment. The kind of substance included and the seriousness of the addiction will direct the course of treatment. Treatment regularly starts with detoxification, utilizing medication to diminish withdrawal indications while a substance leaves the framework. Various social treatment and directing can likewise bolster treatment, serving to deprogram certain practices and conditions identified with drug use.

An individual will set out on a 6-to year restoration program in a devoted office in some cases. Following this, they may live in regulated lodging while they straighten out to overseeing accounts and discovering work. Certain meds can likewise serve to oversee delayed withdrawal side effects and bolster restraint in specific individuals.

For some people, the initial move toward recuperation recognizes their battle with substance reliance. The subsequent stage is finding a treatment program that can help reestablish their general wellbeing, prosperity, and bliss.

There are numerous treatment alternatives an individual can look over. For instance, a few people with severe addiction types enter a detox program before changing into recovery. Others may decide to start recovery at an inpatient or outpatient office. After treatment, it is prescribed to keep strengthening the exercises learned in recovery by helping gatherings and treatment meetings.

Recouping from an addiction isn't simple. It will take a lot of determination and self-restraint to accomplish and keep up long haul moderation. In any case, you're never alone on this excursion.

During recovery, you'll assemble solid associations with others in healing who can identify with what you're experiencing.

Moreover, your family, companions, and friends and family have your eventual benefits on the most fundamental level during this time. Your healing from an addiction is subject to the amount you put into the procedure. Find the manners in which addiction is treated beneath to all the more likely comprehend what lies ahead.

Kinds of Treatment

Treatment programs are diverse for every person and can be modified depending on their unique needs and circumstances. The best sorts of treatment programs guarantee that people in recovery are effectively included at all times.

Inpatient Recovery

Inpatient recoveries offer organized treatment programs intended to address all aspects of a person's addiction.

During inpatient recovery, patients live in a without substance office and get nonstop clinical consideration and helpful help. Inpatient recoveries are the best choice for people engaging in constant addiction, just as the individuals who experience the ill effects of a co-happening mental or social issue.

Outpatient Recovery

Outpatient recoveries are another type of far-reaching addiction care. These projects offer a considerable lot of indistinguishable sorts of effective medications and treatments from inpatient recoveries. In any case, outpatient recoveries permit patients to live at home during the recuperation procedure. Patients can keep working and thinking about their families while going to planned treatment meetings consistently.

It's imperative to remember that outpatient recoveries don't sequester patients from this present reality; hence, patients are in more danger of experiencing triggers that challenge their balance. Along these lines, outpatient recoveries are most appropriate for people with gentle types of addiction and a submitted, restrained way to deal with healing. Outpatient programs are likewise an incredible "advance down" program after inpatient treatment and are regularly joined with calm living homes.

Drug and Alcohol Detox

Detoxification helps individuals securely pull back from their drugs or alcohol until it is never again present in their framework. It is frequently the initial phase in treating people recouping from moderate to severe types of addiction.

Again, detoxing from specific drugs requires medicine to help facilitate the seriousness of withdrawal side effects. Drugs recommended during detox are regularly decreased until the patient is never again genuinely subject to addictive substances.

Calm Living Homes

Calm living homes work as a private extension between an inpatient treatment focus and the arrival to ordinary life. These are beautiful choices for healing individuals who need extra time strengthening what was found out in recovery. Calm living homes help individuals recover fortify their new solid propensities while living in the solace of an organized situation.

Addiction Treatment Meds

During detox and all through treatment, patients might be endorsed meds to help with the recuperation procedure. These meds are utilized for an assortment of purposes, including overseeing withdrawal indications, lessening longings, or treating the co-happening issue. Meds for addiction treatment have the best outcomes when taken related to a specific treatment program.

Instructions to Stage an Intercession

An intercession happens between friends and family and an individual experiencing addiction and is frequently regulated by a mediation pro. The thought behind mediation is to help friends and family productively express their emotions and empower an individual doing combating addiction to enter a treatment program.

Religious Treatment

A few people incline toward a progressively otherworldly way to deal with their healing. Religious recovery places give particular projects and offices that middle around confidence. Inside this kind of recovery program, individuals in recuperation can encircle themselves with similarly invested people searching for direction from a higher capacity to remain stable in the excursion ahead.

Treatments

Treatments utilized in addiction treatment depend on a person's wellbeing and substance misuse designs. Choices for treatment incorporate various individual or gathering treatment meetings, which are commonly sorted out by addiction instructors.

Biofeedback Treatment

Biofeedback is a type of sans drug treatment that enables individuals in healing to comprehend their body's automatic procedures. During a biofeedback meeting, an advisor places electronic sensors on a patient's skin to screen their mind movement. In the wake of surveying mind wave designs, the advisor can suggest a scope of cognitive systems that can be utilized to help beat addictions.

Psychological Conduct Treatment

Psychological conduct treatment (CBT) is utilized to help individuals in recovery reveal risky musings or emotions that may bargain their restraint or add to backslide. This type of treatment is likewise valuable in treating co-happening conditions, for example, bipolar confusion.

Argumentative Conduct Treatment

During argumentative social treatment (DBT), severe psychological instabilities, such as the top enthusiastic issue, are treated as substance use issues. This treatment means developing confidence, giving pressure to the board aptitudes, and urging people to recuperate triggers from their lives.

Experiential Treatment

The experiential treatment uses non-customary treatment strategies to help recuperating addicts defeat stifled sentiments and feelings that may have added to their addiction. Fundamental sorts of this treatment incorporate outside recreational exercises, for example, rock-climbing.

All-encompassing Treatment

Inside all-encompassing treatment, the emphasis is on the person's general prosperity while also treating withdrawal's physical side effects.

Comprehensive treatments may incorporate yoga, needle therapy, and artistry treatment, and guided contemplation.

Persuasive Improvement Treatment

Persuasive improvement treatment (MET) is utilized to help people recuperate how to change any contrary contemplations and practices joined to their addiction. This kind of treatment is often used to treat individuals in substance misuse recuperation who have co-happening conditions, for example, bipolar turmoil and post-horrendous pressure issue (PTSD).

Psychodynamic Treatment

Psychodynamic treatment assists people with investigating their feelings to reveal how their subliminal contemplations identify with their addiction. This assists in distinguishing the hidden reason for substance use. By working intimately with advisors to recognize these profound situated emotions, people are substantially more arranged to distinguish and keep away from enticements during their continuous recuperation.

Care Groups

In the wake of completing an addiction treatment program, it is energetically suggested that a patient join a care group. Care groups are an instrumental piece of remaining on the correct way once out of treatment, taking into account long haul proceeded with care after recovery. The people you meet in help gatherings can offer support all through the recuperation procedure.

There are various diverse care groups custom-fitted to explicit substances or socioeconomics. Finding the correct gathering gives a network of people that propel and motivate each other to remain focused on restraint.

12-Advance Projects

12-advance projects are viewed as the standard for recouping from an addiction. These projects follow the 12-advance model of recovery and the 12 customs made by the authors of Alcoholics Unknown. Since the program permits individuals to adjust the means to their own needs, many have discovered the 12 stages hugely supportive during their recovery.

The most well-known sorts of 12-advance projects are Alcoholics Unknown and Opiates Mysterious.

Alcoholics Unknown

Alcoholics Unknown (AA) gatherings give a gathering of people that would all be able to identify with each other in some way or another about their addiction to alcohol and how it has affected their lives.

Most AA gatherings happen day by day or week after week in a neighborhood setting, for example, a congregation or network building.

Open gatherings energize relatives or friends and family to join in, while shut gatherings are just for healing themselves.

Opiates Unknown

Opiates Unknown (NA) is a care group demonstrated after Alcoholics Mysterious that gives a network of help to those recuperating from an addiction to drugs. Individuals from NA inspire each other to remain focused on moderation and abstain from falling into misuse examples. Gatherings commonly include people sharing their accounts of addiction and recovery.

Extra Treatment Data

Top Alcohol and Drug Recovery Focuses

It's reasonable to feel overpowered when attempting to choose the best recovery program for you or a friend or family member. While there are numerous to browse, there are many eminent drug and alcohol addiction recovery offices that stand apart among others in the country.

These focuses are perceived for the constructive effect in individuals' lives in healing and their families, just like their addiction treatment support endeavors.

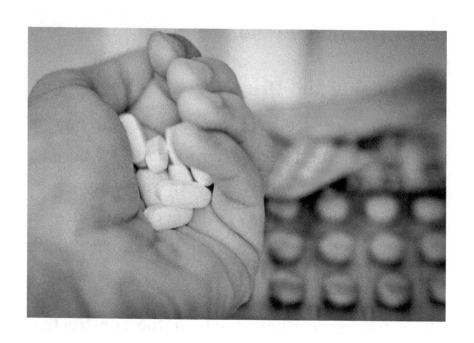

CPSIA information can be obtained
at www.ICGtesting.com
Printed in the USA
LVHW021059260521
688445LV00003B/258

9 781802 740158